THE STORY OF THE NEGRO LEAGUES

By Bo Smolka

Content Consultant
Raymond Doswell, Ed.D.
Curator, Negro Leagues Baseball Museum

Published by ABDO Publishing Company, PO Box 398166, Minneapolis, MN 55439.
Copyright © 2013 by Abdo Consulting Group, Inc. International copyrights reserved
in all countries. No part of this book may be reproduced in any form without written
permission from the publisher. SportsZone™ is a trademark and logo of ABDO
Publishing Company.

Printed in the United States of America,
North Mankato, Minnesota
052012
092012

Editor: Chrös McDougall
Series Designer: Emily Love

Photo Credits
SDN-009529/Chicago History Museum, cover, 1; Bettmann/Corbis / AP Images, 10;
The Abbott Sengstacke Family Papers/Robert Abbott Sengstacke/Getty Images, 12;
Mark Rucker/Transcendental Graphics, Getty Images, 17; HO/AP Images, 18; The
American Museum of Natural History/AP Images, 20; Negro Leagues Baseball Museum,
25; Negro Leagues Baseball Museum, 27; Negro Leagues Baseball Museum, 5, 25, 27,
29, 38, 60; Mark Rucker/Transcendental Graphics, Getty Images, 31; HO/AP Images,
34; AP Images, 36, 41, 46, 48, 55; Eric Risberg/AP Images, 44; Gene J. Puskar/AP
Images, 57

Design elements: Patricia Hofmeester/Shutterstock Images; Bryan Solomon/
Shutterstock Images

Library of Congress Cataloging-in-Publication Data
Smolka, Bo, 1965-
  The story of the Negro leagues / Bo Smolka.
    p. cm. -- (The Negro baseball leagues)
  Includes bibliographical references.
  ISBN 978-1-61783-510-0
  1. Negro leagues--History--Juvenile literature. 2. African American baseball players--
Juvenile literature. 3. Baseball--United States--History--Juvenile literature. I. Title.
  GV875.A1S58 2013
  796.357'64--dc23
                          2012005979

TABLE OF CONTENTS

1

THE EAST-WEST ALL-STAR GAME

James "Cool Papa" Bell stood on second base. Josh Gibson was on first. George "Mule" Suttles was at bat, with 25,000 fans at Comiskey Park in Chicago, Illinois, on their feet.

The fans had already watched some of the best baseball players in the country battle back and forth for 10 innings at the 1935 East-West All-Star Game. They had already witnessed two thrilling comebacks. The East team had taken a 4–0 lead after five innings. The West scored three runs in the sixth and one in the seventh to tie the score at 4–4.

James "Cool Papa" Bell was one of the Negro Leagues' greatest stars, but most people in the United States knew nothing of him.

On through nine innings they played, still tied. In the top of the 10th inning, the East team knocked home four runs. That gave it an 8–4 lead. Yet back came the West again in the bottom of the 10th. As stunned fans watched, the West rallied with four runs. The game was tied yet again at 8–8.

And then came the bottom of the 11th inning. With Bell on second base and two outs, the East team decided to walk Gibson, one of the best power hitters in baseball.

Right-hander Martin Dihigo was on the mound for the East team. Next up for the West team was Suttles, a mountain of a man with hands like bear paws. Dihigo watched Suttles walk to the plate. Dihigo pitched. Suttles took a big swing. Foul ball. Dihigo fired home again. Another big swing, another foul. Dihigo got set and pitched again. This time, Suttles connected. He drove the ball to deep right-center field. Going . . . going . . . gone! Suttles's three-run home run gave the West an 11–8 win in an all-star game classic.

MARTIN DIHIGO

Martin Dihigo could play any position and play it well. In fact, he was the starting center fielder in the 1935 East-West All-Star Game before he came in to pitch. Dihigo was not African-American. He was a native of Cuba. The discrimination that kept blacks from playing Major League Baseball also extended to dark-skinned Cubans such as Dihigo. Walter "Buck" Leonard, a future Hall of Famer, called Dihigo "the greatest all-around player I've ever seen." Playing in the Mexican League in 1938, Dihigo won the batting title with an average of .387. He was also 18–2 as a pitcher with an earned-run average (ERA) of 0.90. Dihigo is in the national baseball halls of fame in the United States, Cuba, and Mexico.

OUT OF SIGHT

Much of America, though, knew nothing of this game. Much of America knew nothing of these players. That is because the East-West Game was the Negro Leagues all-star game. And white America pretty much ignored the Negro Leagues. Virtually every person at Comiskey Park that day, from the ballplayers to the fans to the ushers to the sportswriters, was black.

At that time, the United States was still a very segregated society. Whites and blacks interacted very little. In many places, blacks were not permitted in certain hotels, or restaurants, or stores. This was especially common in the South. It was known as the Jim Crow era. As a result, blacks worshiped at blacks-only churches. They sent their children to blacks-only schools. They sat in blacks-only sections of theaters. This segregation extended to baseball.

Since 1900, no major or minor league baseball team in the United States would sign black players. So the top black players joined non-white teams. In 1935, the Negro National League (NNL) had eight teams stretching from New York to Chicago. Two years earlier, sportswriters Roy Sparrow of the *Pittsburgh Sun-Telegraph* and Bill Nunn of the *Pittsburgh Courier,* two newspapers that catered to black readers, proposed a Negro Leagues all-star game.

With the help of William "Gus" Greenlee, one of the most influential owners in the league, the annual all-star game was established in Chicago. The first East-West Game was held in 1933. That is the same year Major League Baseball (MLB) held its first All-Star Game.

NEGRO LEAGUES

When people talk about the Negro Leagues, they are usually referring to the time between 1920, when the first Negro National League formed, and the late 1950s, when the last Negro Leagues faded away. The end came not long after blacks began playing in the major leagues. Everything before 1920 is often referred to as "independent ball."

The East-West Game proved to be a huge hit. Fans voted for the teams by mailing ballots found in newspapers read by blacks, such as the *Chicago Defender* and *Pittsburgh Courier*. The voting proved to be wildly popular. Technically, blacks had been allowed to vote in US elections since 1870. But many states, especially in the South, made voting difficult for blacks. In some places, blacks had to pay to vote. Many could not afford to do so. Sometimes blacks had to prove they could read or that they knew the US Constitution. Often, whites in the same area did not have to prove that.

These rules have all since been made illegal. But during the 1930s, voting was so difficult for blacks that many did not bother. So the chance to vote for the East-West All-Star Game players was a big deal. More than 17 million ballots were submitted for the 1939 East-West Game. Fans felt involved in the process.

"That was a pretty important thing for black people to do in those days, to be able to vote, even if it was just for ballplayers," Negro Leagues star John "Buck" O'Neil said.

FULL HOUSE

During World War II, the East-West All-Star Game proved to be much more popular than the MLB All-Star Game. Every year from 1942 to 1948, the attendance at the East-West Game was higher than at the MLB All-Star Game. (There was no MLB All-Star Game in 1945.)

Just being able to go to the games was important for many black people during the 1930s. White workers replaced many blacks in unskilled jobs during the Great Depression. That made it hard for black fans to buy tickets to the Negro Leagues baseball games. As a result,

Much of the United States was segregated until the 1960s.

there was little money to run the teams or to pay players. But the players represented success to the black community.

"More than anything else, our games gave black Americans hope all across the country," Negro Leagues star Monte Irvin said. "They said, 'If these ballplayers can succeed under very difficult conditions, then maybe we can too.'"

A PATH TO SOMETHING MORE

The East-West All-Star Game grew to be the social and sporting event of the year for black America. Families scheduled vacations in Chicago, where this game was always held, so they could attend. Trains going to Chicago the week of the game added extra cars. Black fans, celebrities, and politicians all flocked to Chicago. "If you were anybody, you were at the East-West Game," O'Neil recalled.

Many players considered a spot in the East-West Game to be the highlight of their careers. In 1943, a record crowd of more than 51,000 people attended the East-West Game. That was more than attended the MLB All-Star Game. That day, pitcher Leroy "Satchel" Paige threw three no-hit innings for the West. The West won 2–1 despite a ninth-inning home run by the East's Walter "Buck" Leonard. Paige and Leonard were two of the six players on the field that day who would later be inducted into the National Baseball Hall of Fame.

ACCOMMODATIONS

During the era of segregation, blacks—even black baseball stars—were never guaranteed a place to stay while on the road. Finding a hotel was usually easier in bigger cities and in the North. If not, sometimes locals would let a few of the black players stay with them. Otherwise, the players often had to sleep on the bus. Getting food could be just as difficult, as many restaurants and stores would not serve blacks.

By then, the white media—and baseball executives—had started taking notice. They began to see, many for the first time, the talents of these players. Many people believe the East-West Game helped pave the way for blacks to play in the major leagues.

The East-West Game was held every year until 1953. By then, Jackie Robinson and other blacks had broken the color barrier, as it was called. Blacks were playing alongside whites on the famous MLB teams such as the Brooklyn Dodgers, New York Giants, Cleveland Indians, and Chicago White Sox. Many major league scouts attended the East-West Game during its final years. They were hoping to spot the next up-and-coming Negro Leagues star.

They had finally realized what many Negro Leagues followers had said all along: The East-West Game featured some of the best players in baseball history.

The mostly black crowd watches the 1938 East-West All-Star Game at Comiskey Park in Chicago.

2

THE EARLY YEARS

Abner Doubleday is credited with inventing baseball in 1839 in a cow pasture in Cooperstown, New York. Many experts say that is not correct. Several rules of baseball that are credited to Doubleday were already being used in a game called town ball. In the 1930s, the oldest known baseball was found near Cooperstown. That seemed to support Doubleday's role in the game's birth. Another theory suggested baseball was being played during the 1790s in Pittsfield, Massachusetts. The truth might never be known.

What is known is that as far back as the early 1800s, men and boys, black and white, were playing baseball.

For many decades before and during the formation of early baseball, Africans had been captured and brought to the United States. They were forced to work under slavery. The white owners treated the black slaves as property. Slaves were required to do backbreaking work such as picking cotton in their owners' fields. As an escape from their difficult lives, some slaves turned to baseball. Black slave boys sometimes played with the white children of slave owners. One former slave, interviewed during the 1930s, remembered that "always on Saturday afternoon you would have 'till 'first dark' for baseball."

Slavery in the United States ended when the Civil War ended in 1865. By that time, the popularity of baseball was growing very fast in the United States' cities and rural areas.

On June 19, 1846, a group called the

PAY DAY

During the 1880s, Cuban Giants players were paid $12 to $20 per week. "They were the happiest set of men in the world," wrote author Sol White, who played for the Cuban Giants. "Not one would have changed his position with the president of the United States."

New York Knickerbockers had played another New York club in Hoboken, New Jersey. It was the first officially recorded baseball game. Even before the Civil War, black baseball teams were forming in the North, where slavery was ending as an institution. In 1859, the first known or recorded game between all-black teams took place in New York. The Henson Base Ball Club of Queens faced the Weeksville Unknowns from Brooklyn.

One of the best early all-black teams was the Pythian Club in Philadelphia. In 1869, the Pythians played an all-white

"CHIEF TOKAHOMA"

The top black players in the early 1900s proved they could play with the top white players. One of those was Charlie Grant. He was a light-skinned second baseman who had played for two all-black teams in Illinois. John McGraw was the new manager with MLB's Baltimore Orioles. He was impressed when he saw Grant play. He wanted to sign him before the 1901 season. But by then, blacks were not welcome in organized baseball.

McGraw tried to claim that Grant was a "full-blooded Cherokee Indian" named Chief Tokahoma. But one day at an exhibition game in Chicago, many black fans recognized Grant. Charlie Comiskey, the owner of the Chicago White Sox, was not fooled, either. Chief Tokahoma, Comiskey said, was simply Charlie Grant "fixed up with war paint and a bunch of feathers." Facing pressure from the rest of the league, McGraw gave up on the idea of signing Grant.

The Baltimore Blues Base Ball Club, pictured around 1890

team in the first known game between black and white teams. But the Pythians were subject to the racial discrimination that would haunt baseball for decades. When the Pythians tried to join state and national baseball associations, they were turned away.

Baseball, though, was not totally segregated—yet.

THE FIRST BLACK PLAYERS

In 1878, John "Bud" Fowler, a black man, played for a Massachusetts team in a minor league called the International Association. He is recognized as the first black player in what is known as organized baseball. That includes the major leagues and the minor league teams associated with them.

On May 1, 1884, Moses Fleetwood Walker played catcher for Toledo in the major league American Association. He is widely viewed as the first black major leaguer. He played in a major league game 63 years before Jackie Robinson did.

John Henry "Pop" Lloyd

Black players on these early integrated teams faced many hardships. Fans hurled insults at them. Opposing players tried to hit them with pitches or hurt them when they ran the bases. Even their own teammates often did not support them. In 1887, a minor league team from Syracuse had a black pitcher named Robert Higgins. Several of his teammates had come from the South and were prejudiced against blacks. In Higgins's first regular-season start with Syracuse, the fielders behind him purposely misplayed balls. Higgins and his team lost 28–8. Two of his teammates also refused to sit in a team picture with Higgins in it.

With this kind of discrimination, it is not surprising that the number of blacks in organized baseball was very small. Only approximately 30 blacks played in organized baseball before 1899. By 1900, that number was down to zero.

Many white players worked to keep blacks out of the game. Among the most influential was Adrian "Cap" Anson. Anson was the Chicago White Stockings' manager and star first baseman. In 1886, the New York Giants hoped to sign a black pitcher named George Stovey. Anson furiously objected. In 1887, Stovey was to pitch in an exhibition game against Anson's team. Anson said his team would refuse to play if Stovey played.

Led by Anson and others, there was soon a firm color line in baseball. There was no

JOHN HENRY LLOYD

John Henry "Pop" Lloyd is considered one of the best shortstops in baseball history. Statistics for black players in the early 1900s are often hard to find. But Hall of Fame shortstop Honus Wagner, one of the greatest white players of that era, was once asked who had been the best player in baseball history. "If you mean who in organized baseball my answer would be Babe Ruth; but if you mean all baseball, organized or unorganized, the answer would have to be a colored man named John Henry Lloyd."

The St. Paul Gophers, shown in 1909, were one of the Negro Leagues' best teams during the early years of black baseball.

written rule, but it was understood that blacks would no longer be allowed to play in organized baseball.

ALL-BLACK TEAMS

For the many talented black players, that left two choices. They could join one of the many semiprofessional teams that popped up in towns and villages around the country. Those teams sometimes accepted black players. Or they could join all-black teams. Many of the best did that. One of the best early black teams was known as the Cuban Giants. The players were not from Cuba. They might have picked that name to make people think they were Cuban rather than African-American because Hispanic players were seen as more favorable than black players.

One of the early Cuban Giants was an infielder named Sol White. He later became a player and manager of the Philadelphia Giants. Pitcher Andrew "Rube" Foster was one of the Cuban Giants' best players. After the 1903 season, White lured Foster to join his team. White's Philadelphia Giants were a powerhouse of the early 1900s. Foster and some of the Philadelphia players later moved to Chicago. They joined a team called the Leland Giants. They quickly became one of the best black teams in America. Records were not always kept, but it has been reported that in 1907, the Leland Giants won 110 games and lost 10.

It is for what Foster did later, after he finished playing, that he earned the title "The Father of Black Baseball."

THE PAGE FENCE GIANTS

Many black teams traveled a lot. They went from town to town and played any team that would face them. This was known as barnstorming. One of the first and best barnstorming teams was known as the Page Fence Giants. This team did not even have a home field. It traveled in a private train car. When the team reached a town, the players would ride bicycles to the field to generate interest in their games. In 1895, the Page Fence Giants scheduled 156 games in 112 towns in seven states.

3

THE NEGRO LEAGUES ARE BORN

Black baseball picked up steam during the 1920s. In the early 1900s, life in the American South for blacks was very hard. Jobs were scarce. Money was tight. Blacks faced terrible discrimination in almost all aspects of life. Between 1916 and 1919, as many as 500,000 Southern blacks moved to the North and Midwest. That is where there were factory jobs, other work, and, they hoped, more acceptance. This movement became known as the Great Migration.

Blacks flocked to cities such as Philadelphia, New York, Chicago, and Detroit. And where there were a lot of black people, there were soon black baseball teams.

These teams faced some problems, though. In many cases, racial prejudice prevented blacks from scheduling games or renting fields. The fields were almost all owned by whites. Men known as booking agents handled scheduling and field rentals, but they charged high fees.

THE NEGRO NATIONAL LEAGUE

Andrew "Rube" Foster hated this arrangement. He did not want to have to depend on white booking agents. Black teams, Foster thought, should start their own league. They could schedule games with one another. Foster had been a great pitcher during the early 1900s. By now he was the owner of the powerhouse Chicago American Giants. He knew the owners of many other black teams in the Midwest. Led by Foster, these owners met in Kansas City, Missouri, in February 1920. There, the Negro National League was born.

This new league began with eight teams: the Chicago American Giants, the Chicago Giants, the Cuban Stars, the Kansas City Monarchs, the Detroit Stars, the Indianapolis ABCs, the Dayton Marcos, and the St. Louis Giants. All but one of the teams had black owners. The league faced early

RUBE FOSTER

Andrew "Rube" Foster earned his nickname in 1902, when he reportedly outpitched and beat Philadelphia A's star Rube Waddell. Not only did Foster create the first successful Negro League, but he made several other major contributions to baseball. Foster is credited with helping Hall of Fame pitcher Christy Mathewson learn to throw a screwball, which he called a "fadeaway." When Foster was managing the Chicago American Giants, his team perfected strategies such as the bunt-and-run and the double steal. Foster was inducted into the National Baseball Hall of Fame in 1981.

struggles. Records were not always kept. Travel was hard. Some teams lost money. The Dayton team folded after one season.

Still, the league was a huge step forward for black baseball. Weekend games drew crowds of as many as 10,000.

Black baseball, one Kansas City writer said, was a "source of interest, pride, and race glory." Players such as Oscar Charleston, Wilber "Bullet" Rogan, and "Smokey Joe" Williams became folk heroes to blacks. Top players of the 1920s made more than $400 a month. That was much more than the average worker made in those days. So to American blacks, these were not just baseball players. They were success stories.

After a career as a dominant pitcher, Andrew "Rube" Foster
was instrumental in founding the Negro National League.

MORE NEGRO LEAGUES

During the winter of 1922, six Eastern teams formed the
Eastern Colored League. Edward Bolden led the league. He
was the owner of the powerhouse Hilldale team from Darby,
Pennsylvania, which is near Philadelphia. Many Eastern
teams still preferred barnstorming to traditional league play.

There were many good, white semipro teams in the area willing to play Negro Leagues teams. There were fans interested in watching these games. So Negro Leagues teams could make money playing these games.

Once black baseball had two leagues, fans and black sportswriters began clamoring for a black World Series, just as the major leagues had. In 1924, while the Washington Senators and New York Giants squared off in the major league World Series, the Kansas City Monarchs and the Hilldale club faced off in the first Negro World Series. The Monarchs won, five games to four, with one tie.

A MAJOR LEAGUE BLACK EYE

For many years, Negro Leagues teams played games against major league teams in the off-season. The black teams won many of those games. They beat many white Hall of Fame pitchers, including Lefty Grove, Walter Johnson, and Dizzy Dean. The games created a lot of interest. They also earned a lot of money for the black teams. But baseball commissioner Kenesaw Mountain Landis did not like black teams beating his major league teams. So during the 1920s, he ordered that major league teams could not wear their uniforms for these games. From then on, major league teams were known as "all-star teams" when they played these games. When Rube Foster complained about this, Landis reportedly told him, "Mr. Foster, when you beat our teams, it gives us a black eye."

26

**Future Hall of Famer Wilber "Bullet" Rogan helped the
Kansas City Monarchs win the 1924 Negro World Series.
Rogan was a star pitcher and hitter.**

THE HOMESTEAD GRAYS

One of the best black teams of the 1920s did not initially
join either league. The Homestead Grays were based near
Pittsburgh. In 1920, Cumberland "Cum" Posey bought the
team. He had been the team captain as a player. By 1927, the
Grays played more than 150 games every year.

The Grays drew big crowds. Posey paid the Grays players relatively well. So some of the best Negro Leagues players of the time, such as pitcher "Smokey Joe" Williams and slugger John Beckwith, quit their teams and joined the Grays.

The Grays played mostly against club teams from Ohio and Pennsylvania. Still, they won 43 games in a row in 1926 and 31 in a row in 1927. Sometimes they played Negro Leagues teams, and the Grays usually won. After the major league season ended, the Grays played major league all-star teams. The Grays won many of those games, too.

The 1931 Grays team had five future Hall of Fame players. Scores and statistics were not always kept, so their final won-loss record is unclear. It has been listed as 138–6 and somewhere else as 163–23. The actual record will probably never be known. But in 2007, a survey of black baseball historians named the 1931 Grays the best team in Negro Leagues history.

THE "MULE"

George "Mule" Suttles was a huge man with a huge bat. Suttles was 6 feet 6 inches tall and weighed about 250 pounds. He reportedly used a whopping 50-ounce bat. Most major leaguers today use a bat that weighs from 32 to 36 ounces. When Suttles came to bat, fans would shout, "Kick, Mule, kick!" In 1926, Suttles hit .498 with 27 home runs and 21 triples.

By the mid-1920s, two black leagues were up and running.
The Grays were a smashing success. But the good times did
not last.

MONEY TROUBLES

The 1927 season showed just
how different baseball was for
blacks and whites. The New York
Yankees, led by Babe Ruth and
Lou Gehrig, beat the Pittsburgh
Pirates to win the World Series.
Ruth hit a record 60 home runs
and was the talk of baseball. In
the Negro Leagues, the Chicago
American Giants beat the
Atlantic City Bacharach Giants in
the fourth Negro World Series.
But it was a financial disaster.
Black fans would not, or could
not, support a long series by

George "Mule" Suttles

buying tickets to many games. It was expensive for the teams
to get back and forth between Chicago and Atlantic City,
New Jersey. This would be the last Negro World Series until
the 1940s.

In 1928, the Eastern Colored League collapsed. Big cities still had many more whites than blacks. Almost no whites would pay to watch black teams play each other. And many blacks still could not afford tickets to games. Hilldale's owner said he could make more money by playing white semipro teams. Six Eastern teams, including the Grays, tried to start another league in 1929. It was called the American Negro League. But the new league lasted just one season. Another league also quickly shut down.

And things got worse. In October 1929, the US stock market crashed and the Great Depression began.

FIELDS, FIRE IN DETROIT

Among the many difficulties facing Negro Leagues teams was field conditions. Black teams had to rent ballparks from whites. Many of the fields and bleachers were in terrible condition. Some had been abandoned by white teams. On July 7, 1929, there was a fire at Mack Park, the home field of the Detroit Stars. The grandstand roof collapsed and 100 fans were injured.

Millions of people lost their jobs. Owners did not have money to pay players. Fans had to worry about basic things such as food and clothing. They did not have any extra money to spend on baseball games.

The Chicago American Giants, shown in 1922, were one of the Negro Leagues' top teams during the 1920s.

In 1931, the NNL folded. For the first time since 1920, there was no professional black baseball league in the United States. Two years later, however, the Negro Leagues would be reborn.

4

HARD TIMES, THEN THE HEYDAY

By the early 1930s, two established black baseball leagues had gone out of business. They were the Eastern Colored League and the NNL. A few other attempts to start leagues had gone nowhere.

Because of the Great Depression, teams could hardly afford to pay their players. During one series in June 1932, Hilldale players received only about $2 to $4 per game. Some teams passed a hat at games, asking for donations. The Negro Leagues appeared to be finished.

THE GREATEST NEGRO LEAGUES TEAM?

Then William "Gus" Greenlee stepped forward. Greenlee had managed to make money even during the Depression. He did this in many ways. Not all of them were legal. One of his big moneymakers was a numbers game. That was like a lottery. Greenlee put much of his money into his baseball team, the Pittsburgh Crawfords. Before long, he had built it into one of the greatest Negro Leagues teams of all time.

In 1933, led by Greenlee, a new Negro National League formed. Some teams refused to join. They thought starting a league during the Depression was a bad idea. The new league did have many struggles in its first season. But to the surprise of many, it survived. Much of the credit goes to Greenlee. He lost money on his team, but he was one who could afford that. He even loaned money to other teams. He was determined to make the league work.

By 1935, Greenlee's team was the envy of Negro Leagues baseball. It played in Greenlee Stadium, a ballpark that held 6,000 fans. The ballpark was called "a monument of progress." The Crawfords traveled in a shiny new bus with the team name painted on the side. Greenlee used his deep wallet to sign the best players. There were no contracts binding a player to a team. If a rival offered more money, a player might switch teams, even in midseason.

Many consider the 1935 Pittsburgh Crawfords to be the best Negro Leagues team ever. The roster included five future Hall of Famers.

Greenlee's 1935 Crawfords team included five future Hall of Famers: first baseman Oscar Charleston, third baseman William "Judy" Johnson, center fielder James "Cool Papa" Bell, catcher Josh Gibson, and pitcher Leroy "Satchel" Paige. Paige left the team in midseason to join a team in North Dakota. But the Crawfords still won the league championship.

The Crawfords—and all Negro Leagues teams—continued to play many games that did not count in league standings. Records and statistics were not often kept for these games. But eyewitness accounts and the records that do exist tell a lot about these players. Gibson, the slugging catcher, was known as the Babe Ruth of the Negro Leagues. His teammate, Johnson, said that Gibson hit at least 60 home runs every year he played for the Crawfords. Some of his blasts were the farthest that fans or fellow players had ever seen.

Cool Papa Bell was one of the fastest players and best base stealers in baseball history. He hit .400 at least twice. It is said he stole 175 bases in a span of 200 games. That can never be

TRUJILLO'S "DRAGONES"

In 1937, many Negro Leaguers moved to the Dominican Republic. Some of the best played for Trujillo's Dragones. The country's president, Rafael Trujillo, backed the team. His political rivals were supporting other teams. The president wanted badly for his team to win the league championship. Trujillo paid Satchel Paige $2,500 to join the Dragones. Once Paige got to the Dominican Republic, he called several of his Crawfords teammates. Soon Cool Papa Bell, Josh Gibson, outfielder Sam Bankhead, and pitcher Leroy Matlock had also joined Trujillo's team. The players stayed at a posh country club with a swimming pool. But it was hardly a vacation. They were watched over by armed guards and faced enormous pressure to win. But Trujillo's team did win the league championship.

35

proven, but his speed was legendary. He was so fast, Paige once famously said, that Bell could turn off a light switch and jump into bed before the room was dark.

Bell's playing style was typical of the Negro Leagues. While Ruth and white players were slugging their way to fame with home runs, the Negro Leagues game was built on speed. Strategies like the bunt-and-run and double steal were common.

The Crawfords' spot atop the Negro Leagues did not last long. Greenlee ran into money trouble. In 1937, many of the Crawfords' best players left to play in the Dominican Republic. By 1939, the Crawfords were no more.

A HARD LIFE

Despite its gains, Negro Leagues baseball was still very hard. Ever since the Depression, the pay was low. Teams often traveled in rickety, run-down buses that rattled over bumpy, dusty roads. They played in old, neglected ballparks. The schedule was grueling. Pressed for money, owners scheduled two or sometimes three games a day. In many places, blacks

Pittsburgh Crawfords catcher Josh Gibson was one of the best hitters in Negro Leagues history.

were not allowed in restaurants. They often had to buy food and then eat, and sometimes even sleep, cramped in the bus.

Monte Irvin, who played for a team in Newark, New Jersey, in the 1930s and 1940s, remembered one day when his team was driving through Alabama and stopped to get some food. The café owner would not sell them anything because they were black. Irvin remembered her saying, "Whatever it is [you want], we don't have any."

Abe and Effa Manley

Despite all this, another league, the Negro American League (NAL), was formed in 1937. It included many of the top teams in the Midwest. Among them were the Chicago American Giants and the Kansas City Monarchs.

These teams also continued to play many games outside of their league schedules. Riding their rickety buses, the players would sing and play music to pass the time.

"Most all our baseball teams had singing groups," Negro

Leaguer Walter "Buck" Leonard recalled. "It would kill our worries and our tiredness to sing as we went from one town to another at night." Then they would hop off the bus wherever there was a game to be played and money to be made.

One such place was Denver, Colorado. Every year, the *Denver Post* tournament attracted top semipro teams from all over the country. The winning team received $7,500. In 1934, the Monarchs became the first Negro Leagues team invited to the tournament. That year, the Monarchs finished second. (The winning team, an integrated club from Michigan, featured Paige. He was signed just for the tournament.) Almost every year after 1934, a team of Negro

"QUEEN OF THE NEGRO LEAGUES"

Effa Manley showed that she could make it in a man's world. Effa and her husband, Abe, were the owners of the Newark Giants. While Abe handled on-field affairs, Effa worked as the team's business manager and promoter. Effa Manley had a white mother but was raised by a black stepfather and considered herself African-American. She was a vocal supporter of civil rights. She demanded respect for the Negro Leagues and for her players. In 2006, she was inducted in the National Baseball Hall of Fame. As of 2012, she was the only woman enshrined.

Leaguers won the *Denver Post* tournament. That showed fans, and many major league scouts, that the Negro Leagues had some of the best baseball players in the country.

The Monarchs remained one of the most successful Negro Leagues franchises into the 1940s. But in 1946, the fortunes of that team, and the Negro Leagues themselves, changed forever.

FIRST NIGHT GAMES

In 1930, Kansas City Monarchs owner J. L. Wilkinson created a system of portable lights and his team began playing night games. This was five years before the first major league night game. Some people think Wilkinson's creation saved the Negro Leagues. One Friday night game in Detroit in 1930 drew 7,000 fans, a record at that time for a weekday game.

Leroy "Satchel" Paige, considered one of the Negro Leagues' greatest players, played for at least eight teams from 1926 to 1950. Among those teams was the Kansas City Monarchs.

5

THE SUN SETS ON THE NEGRO LEAGUES

Negro Leagues baseball might have never been more popular than in the early 1940s. The United States entered World War II in 1941. Factories needed a lot of workers. Many blacks moved to cities for these jobs. With jobs and more money, black fans could once again buy tickets to games. Attendance at Negro Leagues games soared in the 1940s. At the same time, attendance at MLB games fell sharply. One reason was that many major league stars were serving in the military. But some of the most famous Negro Leagues players were too old to join the military. So they played on, and fans flocked to see them.

The top teams at that time were the Homestead Grays in the East and the Kansas City Monarchs in the West. Led by Josh Gibson and Walter "Buck" Leonard, the Grays won nine straight NNL titles from 1937 to 1945. During the 1940s, the Grays arranged to play some home games in Washington DC. That proved to be a great move. The black population in Washington was growing fast. Fans there were hungry for Negro Leagues baseball. The Grays rented Griffith Stadium, used by the major league Washington Senators. The Senators were usually awful, and the Grays usually drew more fans than the Senators did. A game

CLOWNING AROUND

Negro Leagues baseball teams often used comedy routines to entertain crowds. Some people thought this made the players and their game less serious. Others thought it helped teams draw more fans. That meant more money. One team that did this was called the Indianapolis Clowns. Among their stunts: the catcher would play in a rocking chair, a player would shoot off a firecracker in his glove when he caught the ball, or a player would throw confetti into the crowd. Some of the tricks were similar to those used by the Harlem Globetrotters basketball team. "The fans ate it up," said Hank Aaron. He played for the Clowns for one season.

The Homestead Grays were sometimes more popular than MLB's Washington Senators during the early 1940s.

in June 1942 between the Grays and Monarchs drew close to 30,000 fans.

The Monarchs continued to be the dominant team in the West. Thousands of fans flocked to Monarchs' games on a Sunday. They would be dressed in their Sunday best as they ate barbecue and watched their baseball heroes. Between 1923 and 1955, the Monarchs won 17 league titles. Leroy "Satchel" Paige, one the biggest names in the Negro Leagues, joined the Monarchs for much of the 1940s. The Monarchs' first baseman was John "Buck" O'Neil. Long after his career ended, he traveled the country telling about life in the Negro Leagues.

Interest in the Negro Leagues continued to grow. More and more white fans were watching. So were white sportswriters, some for the first time. Many came away impressed.

H. G. Salsinger was the sports editor of the *Detroit News*. In 1941, he watched a doubleheader between the Baltimore Elite Giants and the Monarchs. "Here was a chance to compare the play of the colored leaguers with that of the major leaguers," Salsinger wrote, "and the comparison, made after more than five hours of competition, was in favor of the colored players."

People were asking why blacks were not allowed to play in the major leagues. Even the new commissioner of baseball, Albert "Happy" Chandler, joined in. Chandler pointed out that blacks were fighting for the United States in the war. If they could serve and die for the country in war, Chandler and others figured, they should be able to play organized baseball.

INTEGRATION AT LAST

Many of the Negro Leaguers had expected that blacks would soon be permitted to join the major leagues. And once black players were allowed, they hoped one of the top Negro Leagues teams, such as the Monarchs or Grays, would join MLB as a team. That did not happen.

FELLER-PAIGE MATCHUPS

After World War II, major league pitcher Bob Feller and Satchel Paige organized a national tour of all-star teams. Feller's all-star team played against a Negro Leagues all-star team led by Paige. The games were wildly popular. The teams played 32 games in 26 days and drew more than 400,000 fans.

Instead, the Brooklyn Dodgers signed a young infielder named Jackie Robinson to a contract in 1945. He had been a star athlete in college. He played one season for the Monarchs. Then, in 1946, Robinson played with the Dodgers' top minor league team. On April 15, 1947, Robinson played first base

Leroy "Satchel" Paige of the Kansas City Monarchs talks with St. Louis Cardinals pitcher Dizzy Dean prior to a 1942 game between the Monarchs and Dean's All-Stars.

In 1947, Jackie Robinson broke through MLB's long-standing color line when he played for the Brooklyn Dodgers.

for the Dodgers. That made him the first black man since the 1800s to play in a major league game.

The color line was broken. It was perhaps the most important event in baseball history. But it also marked the beginning of the end for the Negro Leagues. Over the next few years, a few more blacks joined the majors. Paige and Larry Doby both joined the Cleveland Indians. Soon, black fans were buying tickets to see Robinson or Paige play. Many stopped going to Negro Leagues games.

Even the black newspapers focused on Robinson and Brooklyn. Attendance at Negro Leagues games plummeted. "We couldn't draw flies," the Grays' Buck Leonard said. The Newark Eagles had 120,000 paid fans in 1946. Two years later, they drew 35,000.

After the 1948 season, the NNL folded. The last Negro World Series was held that season. The Homestead Grays beat the Birmingham Black Barons, four games to one. The Black Barons that season featured a gangly 17-year-old who had just finished his sophomore year of high school. Some scouts said they had never seen anyone better. In fact, he became one of the greatest outfielders of all time. His name was Willie Mays.

ROBINSON IN THE NEGRO LEAGUES

Jackie Robinson played the 1945 season with the Kansas City Monarchs. That was his only season in the Negro Leagues. According to the available statistics, he hit .387 that year with five home runs and 13 stolen bases.

MISSED OPPORTUNITIES

A few other Hall of Famers played in the final days of the Negro Leagues. Hank Aaron became MLB's home-run king. Long before that, he was an 18-year-old shortstop with the Indianapolis Clowns. Ernie Banks, who became known as "Mr. Cub" while playing for the Chicago Cubs, was first a star shortstop with the Monarchs.

Many great players never got that chance. James "Cool Papa" Bell, Buck Leonard, and other Negro Leagues stars were ending their careers by the time blacks were allowed in the

NEGRO LEAGUES ROSTERS RAIDED

A problem quickly arose as black players began signing with major league teams. At first, the major league teams did not give the Negro Leagues teams any money for taking these players. They basically just swooped in and took them. These were usually the best and most popular players for their Negro Leagues teams. So not only did the Negro Leagues teams lose some of their best players, but with those players gone, the Negro Leagues teams also continued to lose fans. When one of the Homestead Grays signed with the Brooklyn Dodgers, Grays owner Cumberland "Cum" Posey called Dodgers president Branch Rickey a "thief and robber." In Kansas City, several Monarchs players moved to major league teams. Monarchs owner J. L. Wilkinson received little or nothing in return.

majors. Major league teams thought the players were too old to help.

Ray Dandridge was considered the best Negro Leagues third baseman ever. The New York Giants signed him in 1949. Dandridge played for the Giants' top minor league team in Minneapolis, Minnesota. He hit .362 and was a sparkling fielder. He played for Minneapolis of the American Association again the next season and was the league's Most Valuable Player. But the Giants never promoted him to the major leagues. Some people think that was because he was so popular in Minneapolis. But many people think it was because the Giants already had two black players and did not want a third.

> "The major leagues were easy for me. I learned baseball the hard way. The Negro Leagues made me."
>
> —*Hall of Famer Willie Mays*

"I just would have liked to have been up there for one day," Dandridge said, "even if it was only to get a cup of coffee."

6

IN THE LIMELIGHT, FINALLY

By 1958, the NAL was down to four teams. A few teams continued to barnstorm into the 1960s. For the most part, however, the Negro Leagues were done. They had been a vital presence in black America for more than half a century. But now their story was over.

For many years afterward, these leagues were pretty much forgotten. The tales of colorful, talented men who played in them—guys with names like Smokey Joe, Cool Papa, Mule, and Turkey—had vanished.

Ray Dandridge, the great third baseman, said that years after he finished playing, "I'd go out on the street and the kids didn't know a thing about our Negro baseball."

CREATING A LEGACY

The first push to recognize these players came from Ted Williams. He played for the Boston Red Sox and is considered one of the greatest hitters of all time. He was inducted into the National Baseball Hall of Fame in 1966. In his Hall of Fame speech, Williams said, "I hope someday Satchel Paige and Josh Gibson will be voted into the Hall of Fame as symbols of the great Negro players who are not here only because they were not given the chance."

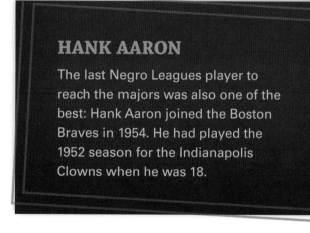

HANK AARON

The last Negro Leagues player to reach the majors was also one of the best: Hank Aaron joined the Boston Braves in 1954. He had played the 1952 season for the Indianapolis Clowns when he was 18.

Then, a few years later, Robert Peterson wrote a book called *Only the Ball Was White*. It was one of the first books about the Negro Leagues. In 1970, the Hall of Fame had virtually no records, documents, or other evidence from the

Negro Leagues. It was as if half the sport's history in the United States had never existed.

Bowie Kuhn became baseball commissioner in 1969. He promoted the idea of Negro Leaguers in the Hall of Fame. Some members of the Hall disagreed. Their reason? Hall of Fame players must have played 10 years in the major leagues. But many of these Negro Leaguers were never allowed in the major leagues. That should not count against them, Kuhn and others argued.

Finally, the Hall of Fame announced it would have a special exhibit about the Negro Leagues. But fans and Negro Leagues players were still angry. Peterson argued that these players did not belong in "some obscure corner of the museum." Paige said, "I was just as good as the white boys. I ain't going in the back door of the Hall of Fame."

"Everyone says, 'Isn't it a shame that Satchel Paige didn't play with all the great athletes of the major leagues?' But who's to say he didn't, playing with us?"

—*John "Buck" O'Neil*

Then, in 1971, the Hall of Fame announced that Paige would receive full induction. He was the first Negro Leaguer honored that way. Over the next five years, several others, including Gibson, James "Cool Papa" Bell, and Walter "Buck" Leonard, were inducted. But many more were left out.

Negro Leagues first baseman Walter "Buck" Leonard poses with
MLB commissioner Bowie Kuhn after being inducted into the
National Baseball Hall of Fame in 1972.

REMEMBERING THE NEGRO LEAGUES

In 1994, the documentary film *Baseball* by Ken Burns brought
the Negro Leaguers to life for millions of viewers. More and
more books and movies on the subject were produced. In 1997,
an expanded exhibit on the Negro Leagues opened at the Hall
of Fame. That same year the Negro Leagues Baseball Museum
moved into a larger building in Kansas City. The story of the
amazing players of this era is finally being told.

In 2006, a special committee announced that 17 people
from the Negro Leagues would be inducted into the Hall of

Fame. One person who was not chosen among the 17 was John "Buck" O'Neil. People were furious about this. O'Neil had spent much of his life promoting the Negro Leagues. He was a major force behind the creation of the Negro Leagues Baseball Museum. Then, in 2008, the Hall of Fame announced that it had created the Buck O'Neil Lifetime Achievement Award.

For O'Neil, Gibson, and countless other players, there will never be total justice. These players should have had a chance to play in the major leagues and did not. Jim Crow laws and the discrimination of that time in the United States will always be a shameful part of the country's history. But the players of the Negro Leagues are finally receiving their due.

Many Negro Leagues stars, later in their lives, looked back on their baseball careers fondly. Many were able to look past the unfairness and the racism and the hatred.

PITTSBURGH

Pittsburgh, Pennsylvania, was one of the most important cities in Negro Leagues history. Both the Crawfords and the Homestead Grays played there. They were two of the most successful teams in black baseball history. The NNL was restarted there in 1933. In 1988, the Pittsburgh Pirates honored those teams by issuing Crawfords and Grays trading cards. Then in 2006, the Pirates opened Legacy Square, an exhibit in the Pirates' stadium that honors the Negro Leagues and the great players from the Crawfords and Grays.

A statue honoring Negro Leagues great Josh Gibson stands in Legacy Square outside PNC Park, the Pittsburgh Pirates' home ballpark.

They recalled warm summer nights, the sound of a bat hitting a ball, the smell of a leather glove. It is clear that, through all the hardship, they played for the love of the game.

O'Neil captured that spirit when he said, "I feel sorry for the white baseball fans of that era, because they didn't get to see us play. But don't feel sorry for any of us. . . . I played with the greatest ball players in the world. I saw this country and a lot of other countries, and I met a lot of wonderful people. They say, 'Buck, you were just born at the wrong time.' But I say, 'No, I was born right on time.'"

TIMELINE

1859

The Henson Base Ball Club faces the Weeksville Unknowns in the first known baseball game between all-black teams.

1909: OUCH!

In a game against the Chicago Cubs in October, Lelands outfielder Joe Green broke his leg stealing third base. When the throw to third was wild, Green got up and hopped home to score. He then collapsed on the ground and was carried off the field.

1900

No black players are left in Major League Baseball.

1920: WHAT A COMEBACK!

In 1920, the Chicago American Giants were losing to Indianapolis 18–0 in the eighth inning. Using a combination of bunt hits and grand slams, Chicago scored nine runs in the eighth inning and nine in the ninth inning, and the game ended in a tie, 18–18.

1920

The first Negro National League is formed.

1933

The second Negro National League is formed.

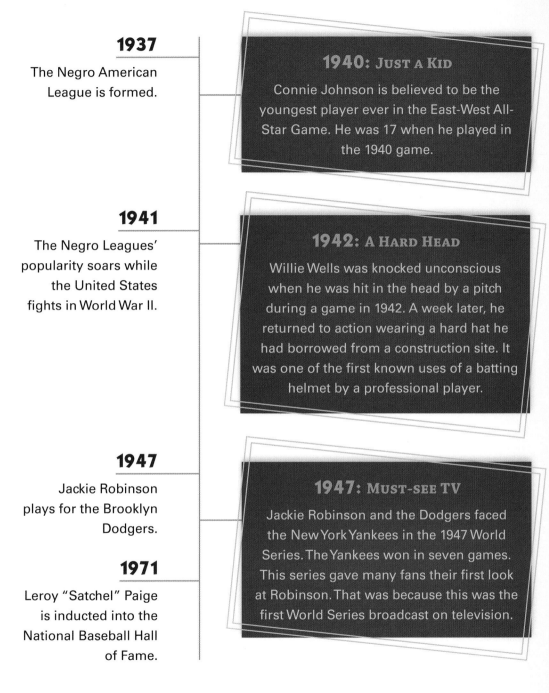

1937

The Negro American League is formed.

1940: Just a Kid

Connie Johnson is believed to be the youngest player ever in the East-West All-Star Game. He was 17 when he played in the 1940 game.

1941

The Negro Leagues' popularity soars while the United States fights in World War II.

1942: A Hard Head

Willie Wells was knocked unconscious when he was hit in the head by a pitch during a game in 1942. A week later, he returned to action wearing a hard hat he had borrowed from a construction site. It was one of the first known uses of a batting helmet by a professional player.

1947

Jackie Robinson plays for the Brooklyn Dodgers.

1947: Must-see TV

Jackie Robinson and the Dodgers faced the New York Yankees in the 1947 World Series. The Yankees won in seven games. This series gave many fans their first look at Robinson. That was because this was the first World Series broadcast on television.

1971

Leroy "Satchel" Paige is inducted into the National Baseball Hall of Fame.

Negro Leagues Baseball Museum

1616 East 18th Street
Kansas City, MO 64108-1610
816-221-1920
www.nlbm.com

The Negro Leagues Baseball Museum preserves the history of Negro Leagues baseball through interactive exhibits, films, photos, sculptures, and artifacts. The museum does not serve as a hall of fame for black baseball. Because the sport is no longer segregated, the Negro Leagues Baseball Museum recognizes the National Baseball Hall of Fame in Cooperstown, New York, as the shrine for all of baseball's greatest players.

The museum opened in 1994 and moved into a new 10,000-square-foot space in 1997. It is located in the historic 18th & Vine Jazz District, a traditional center for black culture in Kansas City. The Paseo YMCA building, where the Negro National League was founded in 1920, is nearby.

GLOSSARY

attendance
The number of fans who attend a game, a series, or a season.

barnstorming
When a team travels around and faces various opponents rather than playing in a traditional league.

color line
An unwritten rule within MLB that prevented black players from playing in the majors until Jackie Robinson joined the Brooklyn Dodgers in 1947.

commissioner
The person in charge of baseball's major and minor leagues.

discrimination
Treating people differently based on prejudice.

doubleheader
A set of two baseball games played between the same two teams on the same day.

exhibition
A game in which the teams play to develop skills and promote the sport rather than for a competitive advantage.

franchise
An entire sports organization, including the players, coaches, and staff.

inducted
Formally added.

media
Various forms of communication, including television, radio, and newspapers; the press or news reporting agencies.

segregation
When groups of people are legally separated from each other.

semiprofessional
A level below professional in which players are paid but not enough to survive on as a full-time job.

slave
Somebody forced to work for another person.

FOR MORE INFORMATION

Select Bibliography

Hogan, Lawrence D. *Shades of Glory*. Washington DC: National Geographic Society, 2006.

Holway, John. *The Complete Book of the Negro Leagues: The Other Half of Baseball History*. Fern Park, FL: Hastings House Publishers, 2001.

Lanctot, Neil. *Negro League Baseball: The Rise and Ruin of a Black Institution*. Philadelphia: University of Pennsylvania Press, 2004.

Lester, Larry. *Black Baseball's National Showcase*. Lincoln, NE: University of Nebraska Press, 2001.

Rogosin, Donn. *Invisible Men: Life in Baseball's Negro Leagues*. Lincoln, NE: University of Nebraska Press, 1983.

Further Readings

Nelson, Kadir. *We Are the Ship: The Story of Negro League Baseball*. New York: Jump at the Sun/Hyperion Books for Children, 2008.

Smith, Charles R. *Stars in the Shadows: The Negro League All-Star Game of 1934*. New York: Atheneum, 2012.

Sturm, James, and Rich Tommaso. *Satchel Paige: Striking Out Jim Crow*. New York: Jump at the Sun, 2007.

Weatherford, Carole Boston. *A Negro League Scrapbook*. Honesdale, PA: Boyds Mills Press, 2005.

Withers, Ernest C. *Negro League Baseball*. New York: Harry N. Abrams, 2004.

Web Links

To learn more about the Negro Leagues, visit ABDO Publishing Company online at **www.abdopublishing.com**. Web sites about the Negro Leagues are featured on our Book Links page. These links are routinely monitored and updated to provide the most current information available.

Places to Visit

Highmark Legacy Square
PNC Park
115 Federal Street
Pittsburgh, PA 15212
412-325-4700
http://pittsburgh.pirates.mlb.com/pit/community/legacysquare.jsp
Located just outside the Pittsburgh Pirates' PNC Park, Highmark Legacy Square offers interactive exhibits dedicated to preserving the history of the Negro Leagues, including the local Homestead Grays and Pittsburgh Crawfords.

National Baseball Hall of Fame
25 Main Street
Cooperstown, NY 13326
888-HALL-OF-FAME
www.baseballhall.org
This hall of fame and museum highlights the greatest players and moments in the history of baseball. Over the last several decades, several former Negro Leaguers have been inducted and enshrined here.

INDEX

About the Author: Bo Smolka is a former sports copy editor at the *Baltimore Sun* and former sports information director at Bucknell, his alma mater. He won several writing awards from the College Sports Information Directors of America, including the National Story of the Year. He lives in Baltimore, Maryland, with his wife and two children. When he is not writing about baseball he can often be found coaching his son's baseball teams.